Learn COBOL

Practical Guide

A. De Quattro

Copyright © 2024

COBOL Guide

1.Introduction to COBOL

COBOL, short for COmmon Business-Oriented Language, is one of the oldest programming languages still in use today. Created in 1959 by a committee of experts led by Grace Hopper, COBOL was primarily designed for processing business and financial data. It is known for its clear and readable syntax and its ability to efficiently handle large amounts of data.

COBOL was one of the first programming languages to be standardized, which contributed to its widespread adoption and longevity. Despite being developed over 60 years ago, COBOL is still widely used in industries such as financial institutions, insurance, public administration, and many other businesses that manage large amounts of data.

One of the distinctive features of COBOL is

its focus on the business aspects of programming. The language is designed to be easily understood even by those without a deep technical background, making it very popular among business analysts and industry experts.

One of the main reasons why COBOL is still widely used is its reliability and stability. Many companies still rely on legacy systems written in COBOL, and it is often more cost-effective to continue using them rather than replacing them with new technologies. Additionally, COBOL can easily integrate with other programming languages and modern technologies, making it a versatile choice for many businesses.

One of the most interesting aspects of COBOL is its ability to efficiently process large amounts of data. Thanks to its batch processing features and its ability to generate output in various formats, COBOL is a powerful tool for creating reports and data analysis.

Another important aspect of COBOL is its portability. The language is supported by a wide range of hardware and software platforms, which means that programs written in COBOL can be run on different systems without substantial modifications.

Despite its longevity, COBOL continues to undergo constant development and updates. In recent years, new features and improvements have been introduced to make the language even more powerful and suitable for the modern needs of businesses.

Ultimately, COBOL remains a fundamental programming language for many companies worldwide. Its reliability, versatility, and ability to handle large amounts of data make it an ideal choice for many business applications and specific industries. Although it may appear outdated compared to more modern technologies, COBOL continues to demonstrate its usefulness and value in today's computing landscape.

2. Structure of a COBOL program

The structure of a COBOL program is divided into different elements that define its organization and functioning.

Let's start with the main elements of a COBOL program:

- IDENTIFICATION DIVISION: in this division, the name of the program and information about the programmer are defined.

- ENVIRONMENT DIVISION: in this division, the resources used by the program are specified, such as input/output files and working variables.

- DATA DIVISION: in this division, the variables used within the program are declared.

- PROCEDURE DIVISION: in this division,

the program logic is written, which includes the instructions that determine the program flow.

Here is an example structure of a COBOL program:

IDENTIFICATION DIVISION.

PROGRAM-ID. EXAMPLE.

AUTHOR. Mario Rossi.

ENVIRONMENT DIVISION.

DATA DIVISION.

WORKING-STORAGE SECTION.

01 SUM PIC 99.

PROCEDURE DIVISION.

INIT-SUM.

 MOVE 10 TO SUM.

 DISPLAY "The value of the sum is: " SUM.

STOP RUN.

In this example, the program is named "EXAMPLE" and was written by Mario Rossi. In the DATA DIVISION, we have declared a working variable called "SUM" of numeric type with two digits. In the PROCEDURE DIVISION, the variable SUM is initialized with the value 10 and the message "The value of the sum is: 10" is displayed on the screen.

This is just an example of the structure of a COBOL program, which can vary depending on the needs and specifications of the application. The key to writing a good COBOL program is clarity and organization, following the rules and conventions of the language.

3. Declaration of variables in COBOL

In COBOL language, variables are defined within a variable declaration section. This section is usually placed at the beginning of a COBOL program and includes the types of variables that will be used in the program.

Variables in COBOL can be of different types, such as whole numbers, decimal numbers, text strings, and Booleans. Each type of variable has a specific format for declaration and usage.

Here are some examples of common variable declarations in COBOL:

1. Declaration of a whole number variable:

```
IDENTIFICATION DIVISION.
```

```
PROGRAM-ID. EXAMPLE.
DATA DIVISION.
WORKING-STORAGE SECTION.
01 INTEGER-NUMBER PIC 9(5).
```
```

In this example, we have declared a variable named INTEGER-NUMBER of type whole number with a length of 5 digits. The "PIC 9(5)" declaration means that the variable can hold up to 5 numeric digits.

2. Declaration of a decimal number variable:
```

```
IDENTIFICATION DIVISION.
PROGRAM-ID. EXAMPLE.
DATA DIVISION.
WORKING-STORAGE SECTION.
01 DECIMAL-NUMBER PIC S9(3)V9(2).
```

```

Here, we have declared a variable named DECIMAL-NUMBER of type decimal number with a whole part of 3 digits and a decimal part of 2 digits. The "S" letter before the declaration indicates the sign of the decimal number.

3. Declaration of a string variable:

```
IDENTIFICATION DIVISION.
PROGRAM-ID. EXAMPLE.
DATA DIVISION.
WORKING-STORAGE SECTION.
01 CUSTOMER-NAME PIC X(30).
```

Here we have declared a variable named
```

CUSTOMER-NAME of type string with a maximum length of 30 characters. The "PIC X(30)" declaration indicates that the variable can hold up to 30 alphanumeric characters.

4. Declaration of a Boolean variable:

```
IDENTIFICATION DIVISION.
PROGRAM-ID. EXAMPLE.
DATA DIVISION.
WORKING-STORAGE SECTION.
01 BOOLEAN PIC X(1).
```

In this example, we have declared a variable named BOOLEAN of type Boolean with a length of 1 character. The variable can take values of "T" or "F" to indicate true or false respectively.

It is also possible to declare complex variables in COBOL, such as arrays and records. For example:

1. Declaration of an array of whole numbers:

```
IDENTIFICATION DIVISION.

PROGRAM-ID. EXAMPLE.

DATA DIVISION.

WORKING-STORAGE SECTION.

01 NUMBER-ARRAY.

   05 NUMBERS OCCURS 10 TIMES PIC 9(3).
```

In this case, we have declared an array named NUMBER-ARRAY containing 10 elements, each of type whole number with a length of 3 digits.

2. Declaration of a record:

```
IDENTIFICATION DIVISION.
PROGRAM-ID. EXAMPLE.
DATA DIVISION.
WORKING-STORAGE SECTION.
01 CUSTOMER-RECORD.
   05 NAME PIC X(30).
   05 SURNAME PIC X(30).
   05 AGE PIC 9(2).
```

Here we have declared a record named CUSTOMER-RECORD with three fields: NAME (30-character string), SURNAME (30-character string), and AGE (whole number with two digits).

Variables in COBOL must be declared before they can be used in the program. It is important to note that each variable must be declared with a unique name and an appropriate data type. Proper usage of variables is essential to ensure the correct execution of the COBOL program.

4. Program control structures (if, else, do, etc.) in COBOL

In COBOL, there are program control structures that allow for precise and flexible management of the execution flow of instructions.

The main program control structures in COBOL include:

- Conditional execution (IF-ELSE-END-IF)

- Iterative execution (PERFORM UNTIL, PERFORM VARYING)

- Execution of a known block of instructions (PERFORM, END-PERFORM)

Conditional execution (IF-ELSE-END-IF):

Conditional execution is one of the most commonly used control structures in COBOL, and allows for executing a block of instructions only if a specific condition is met.

The basic syntax is as follows:

IF condition

  statement 1

ELSE

  statement 2

END-IF

In the following example, a simple conditional execution in COBOL is shown:

```
IDENTIFICATION DIVISION.
PROGRAM-ID. IFELSE_EXAMPLE.

ENVIRONMENT DIVISION.
DATA DIVISION.
WORKING-STORAGE SECTION.
```

```
01 NUMBER PIC 9 VALUE 10.

PROCEDURE DIVISION.
    IF NUMBER = 10
        DISPLAY "The number is 10"
    ELSE
        DISPLAY "The number is not 10"
    END-IF.

    STOP RUN.
```

In this example, a variable NUMBER is defined with an initial value of 10. It then checks if the value of the variable is equal to 10, and displays an appropriate message based on the result.

Iterative execution (PERFORM UNTIL, PERFORM VARYING):

Iterative execution allows for repeating a block of instructions a certain number of times, until a specific condition is met. There are two main ways to implement a loop in COBOL: PERFORM UNTIL and PERFORM VARYING. Here is an example of both:

PERFORM UNTIL:

    IDENTIFICATION DIVISION.

  PROGRAM-ID. PERFORM_UNTIL_EXAMPLE.

    ENVIRONMENT DIVISION.

    DATA DIVISION.

    WORKING-STORAGE SECTION.

    01 COUNTER PIC 9 VALUE 1.

    PROCEDURE DIVISION.

```
PERFORM UNTIL COUNTER > 5
    DISPLAY COUNTER
    ADD 1 TO COUNTER
END-PERFORM.


STOP RUN.
```

In this example, a variable COUNTER is defined with an initial value of 1. It then repeats the block of instructions DISPLAY and ADD 1 TO COUNTER until the variable COUNTER becomes greater than 5.

PERFORM VARYING:

```
IDENTIFICATION DIVISION.
PROGRAM-ID.
PERFORM_VARYING_EXAMPLE.
```

```cobol
ENVIRONMENT DIVISION.

DATA DIVISION.

WORKING-STORAGE SECTION.

01 COUNTER PIC 9 VALUE 1.


PROCEDURE DIVISION.

    PERFORM VARYING COUNTER FROM 1 BY 1 UNTIL COUNTER > 5

        DISPLAY COUNTER

    END-PERFORM.


    STOP RUN.
```

In this example, the PERFORM VARYING structure is used to execute a block of instructions a certain number of times, modifying the value of the variable COUNTER at each iteration.

Execution of a known block of instructions (PERFORM, END-PERFORM):

The PERFORM-END-PERFORM structure is used to execute a known block of instructions a certain number of times. This structure does not have a specific exit condition, but relies on an external control to determine when to stop the execution. Here is an example:

```
IDENTIFICATION DIVISION.
PROGRAM-ID. PERFORM_EXAMPLE.


ENVIRONMENT DIVISION.
DATA DIVISION.
WORKING-STORAGE SECTION.
01 COUNTER PIC 9 VALUE 1.

PROCEDURE DIVISION.
    PERFORM 5 TIMES
```

```cobol
    DISPLAY "Iteration " COUNTER
    ADD 1 TO COUNTER
END-PERFORM.


STOP RUN.
```

In this example, the PERFORM structure is used to execute a block of instructions 5 times, displaying a message at each iteration that includes the current value of the variable COUNTER.

In COBOL, it is possible to combine different program control structures to handle complex and variable situations. For example, conditional execution can be used within an iterative loop to control the execution flow based on multiple conditions.

Program control structures in COBOL are essential for managing the execution flow of instructions in a flexible and efficient manner. They are powerful tools that allow programmers to write complex code in a clear and readable way. With a proper understanding and implementation of these structures, it is possible to create robust and efficient COBOL programs.

5. Use of comments in COBOL code

One of the distinctive features of COBOL is its support for comments in the code, which allows programmers to document and explain their code clearly and understandably.

Comments in COBOL code are textual or allow temporarily disabling parts of the code, allowing programmers to make the code more readable and facilitate code maintenance and understanding. Comments are not interpreted by the COBOL compiler and therefore do not affect the program's execution.

In COBOL, comments can be either inline or multiline. An inline comment starts with the asterisk (*) character and ends at the end of the line. For example:

   MOVE VALUE-1 TO VALUE-2. * Copy the value from the variable VALUE-1 to the variable VALUE-2

For multiline comments, you can use the syntax /* to start the comment and */ to end it. For example:

/*

This is a multiline comment describing

the use of variables VALUE-1 and VALUE-2

*/

The proper use of comments in COBOL code is essential for understanding and maintaining the code. Comments should be used to explain the reason for certain design choices, describe the logic of the code, document program requirements or specifications, and provide instructions or warnings to future programmers who may need to work on the code.

Another way comments can be useful is during code debugging. Programmers can insert temporary comments within the code to temporarily disable parts of it and isolate runtime issues. For example, if a particular piece of code is suspected of causing an error, you can comment out that section of code to see if the program runs correctly without it.

It is important to note that comments in COBOL code should be accurate and up-to-date. It is common for programmers to insert comments in the code during development but then forget about them or not keep them updated while making changes to the code. This can lead to outdated or incomplete documentation, which can complicate code maintenance over time.

To encourage proper and consistent use of comments in COBOL code, many organizations adopt coding guidelines or conventions that define how comments should be formatted and where they should be placed in the code. For example, standards may be defined for the beginning and end of multiline comments, the maximum length of inline comments, the syntax for paragraph or code section comments, and so on.

In conclusion, the use of comments in COBOL code is an essential practice to ensure that the code is clear, documented, and easily maintainable. Comments allow programmers to explain the logic of their code, provide instructions to future maintainers, and simplify the debugging process. It is important for programmers to follow coding guidelines and conventions to ensure that comments are consistent and accurate and that the code is easily understandable and modifiable over time.

6. Declaration and usage of various types of data (alpha, numeric, decimal, etc.) in COBOL

COBOL (Common Business-Oriented Language) is a programming language primarily used for the development of enterprise software and large-scale applications. Born in the 1950s, COBOL is still widely used in sectors such as finance, healthcare, and public administration, where data accuracy and reliability are crucial.

In the COBOL language, data is defined using various data types that represent different types of information. These data types can be divided into different categories, including alphanumeric data, numeric data, and decimal data.

Alphanumeric data in COBOL is used to store character strings, such as names, addresses, descriptions, and other non-numeric information. To define alphanumeric data in COBOL, the "PIC X" data type is used, followed by the desired field length. For example, to define a 20-character long field named "NAME", the following declaration can be used:

```
01 NAME PIC X(20).
```

The "NAME" field can then contain a character string with a maximum length of 20.

Numeric data in COBOL is used to store numeric values, such as amounts, quantities, numeric codes, and other quantitative information. Numeric data can be integers or decimals and can be represented using various data types in COBOL.

To define an integer data in COBOL, the "PIC 9" data type is used, followed by the field length. For example, to define a 5-digit long customer code field named "CUST_CODE", the following declaration can be used:

```
01 CUST_CODE PIC 9(5).
```

The "CUST_CODE" field can then contain an integer value composed of 5 digits.

Decimal data in COBOL is used to store numeric values with decimal precision, such as monetary amounts and financial calculations. To define decimal data in COBOL, the "PIC S9" data type is used, followed by the length of the integer part and the decimal part of the field. For example, to define a "AMOUNT" field composed of 7 digits of integer part and 2 decimal digits, the following declaration can be used:

```
01 AMOUNT PIC S9(7)V99.
```

The "AMOUNT" field can then contain a numeric value with 7 digits of integer part and 2 decimal digits, for example €1234.56.

In addition to alphanumeric, numeric, and decimal data, COBOL also supports other special data types, such as dates, times, and boolean values. To define a date data in COBOL, the "PIC 9(6)" data type is used, with the first two characters representing the year, the next two characters representing the month, and the last two characters representing the day. For example, to define a date field "DATE" in AAAAMMDD format, the following declaration can be used:

```
01 DATE PIC 9(6).
```

The "DATE" field can then contain a date in AAAAMMDD format.

To define a time data in COBOL, the "PIC 9(6)" data type is used, with the first two characters representing the hour, the next two characters representing the minutes, and the last two characters representing the seconds. For example, to define a time field "TIME" in HHMMSS format, the following declaration can be used:

```
01 TIME PIC 9(6).
```

The "TIME" field can then contain a time in HHMMSS format.

To define a boolean data in COBOL, the "PIC X" data type is used, followed by a single character representing the true or false boolean value. For example, to define a boolean field "FLAG" that can take values "Y" for true and "N" for false, the following declaration can be used:

```
01 FLAG PIC X.
```

The "FLAG" field can then contain a true or false boolean value, represented respectively by the characters "Y" and "N".

In addition to data declaration, COBOL allows the use of various types of instructions to manipulate and present data in different ways. For example, to perform arithmetic operations on numeric data, instructions like ADD, SUBTRACT, MULTIPLY, and DIVIDE can be used. To perform comparisons between data, instructions like IF, ELSE, and PERFORM UNTIL can be used. To manipulate character strings, instructions like MOVE, STRING, and UNSTRING can be used.

In conclusion, COBOL is a powerful and flexible programming language that allows the declaration and use of various types of data to handle information of different types and formats. Thanks to its wide availability of data types and instructions, COBOL is still widely used today for the development of critical business applications in sectors where data accuracy and reliability are essential.

7. Data Manipulation in COBOL

Data manipulation in COBOL is a fundamental part of programming in this language, as COBOL is primarily designed to handle operations on structured data in tabular format.

One of the most important aspects of data manipulation in COBOL is the definition of data structures. COBOL supports various primitive data types such as integers, decimals, characters, and booleans, as well as more complex structures like arrays, records, and files. Data declaration is done through the DATA DIVISION paragraph, where the variables used in the program are defined.

For example, to declare a numeric variable, the following syntax is used:

```
```

```
01 NUM-VAR PIC 9(5).
```

In this case, NUM-VAR is the variable name and PIC 9(5) specifies that it is a numeric variable of 5 digits. Furthermore, more complex structures like arrays and records can be defined. For example, to declare an array of 10 integers, the following syntax is used:

```
01 NUM-ARRAY PIC 9(5) OCCURS 10 TIMES.
```

In this case, NUM-ARRAY is the array name and OCCURS 10 TIMES specifies that the array consists of 10 elements, each being a numeric variable of 5 digits. To declare a record with different fields, the following syntax is used:

```
01 STUDENT-RECORD.
   05 STUDENT-ID PIC X(10).
   05 STUDENT-NAME PIC X(20).
   05 STUDENT-AGE PIC 9(2).
```

In this case, STUDENT-RECORD is the record name and the fields STUDENT-ID, STUDENT-NAME, and STUDENT-AGE represent the fields of the record with their respective data types.

Once the data is defined, it can be manipulated within the COBOL program using different statements. The main statements for data manipulation in COBOL are MOVING, ADD, SUBTRACT, MULTIPLY, and DIVIDE. For example, to assign a value to a variable, the MOVING statement is used:

```
MOVE 10 TO NUM-VAR.
```

In this case, the value 10 is assigned to the variable NUM-VAR. To perform mathematical operations between variables, the ADD, SUBTRACT, MULTIPLY, and DIVIDE statements are used:

```
ADD 10 TO NUM-VAR.

SUBTRACT 5 FROM NUM-VAR.

MULTIPLY NUM-VAR BY 2.

DIVIDE NUM-VAR BY 3.
```

These statements respectively perform addition, subtraction, multiplication, and division between the variable NUM-VAR and a specified value.

It is also possible to manipulate arrays and records using specific COBOL statements. For example, to access an element of an array, the index of the desired element is used:

```
```

MOVE 20 TO NUM-ARRAY(5).
```
```

In this case, the value 20 is assigned to the fifth position of the array NUM-ARRAY. To access the fields of a record, the indices specified in the record declaration are used:

```
```

```
MOVE "12345" TO STUDENT-ID.
MOVE "John Doe" TO STUDENT-NAME.
MOVE 25 TO STUDENT-AGE.
```

In this case, values are assigned to the fields of the STUDENT-RECORD.

Another important aspect of data manipulation in COBOL is file handling. COBOL supports input/output operations on sequential files and indexed files. To open a file in COBOL, the OPEN statement is used:

```
OPEN INPUT FILE-NAME.
OPEN OUTPUT FILE-NAME.
```

Where FILE-NAME is the name of the file to open, and INPUT specifies that the file is opened in read mode, while OUTPUT specifies that the file is opened in write mode.

Once the file is opened, data can be read and written using the READ and WRITE statements:

```
READ FILE-NAME INTO DATA-RECORD.
WRITE DATA-RECORD.
```

Where DATA-RECORD is the record containing the file data. The READ statement reads a record from the file and stores it in the DATA-RECORD, while the WRITE statement writes the DATA-RECORD to the file.

Furthermore, specific statements can be used for searching and sorting data in indexed files. To perform a search within an indexed file, the READ statement with the KEY option is used:

```
READ FILE-NAME
  KEY IS KEY-VALUE
  INVALID KEY
    DISPLAY "KEY NOT FOUND"
  END-READ.
```

In this case, KEY-VALUE represents the key value to search for in the indexed file.

Finally, data manipulation in COBOL can be optimized using advanced techniques such as using success/error indicators, exception handling, and performance optimization through the use of indexing and sorting. By utilizing these techniques, efficient and robust COBOL programs can be created for data manipulation.

Data manipulation in COBOL is an essential part of programming in this language. With the correct procedures and techniques, it is possible to efficiently and securely manage operations on structured data, ensuring the correctness and reliability of the manipulated data.

8. Using arrays and tables in COBOL

COBOL (Common Business-Oriented Language) is a programming language designed primarily for processing business data and commercial transactions on mainframes. One of the most commonly used tools in COBOL for organizing and managing data is represented by arrays and tables.

Arrays are an ordered collection of elements of the same data type, which are stored in a contiguous sequence of memory. Tables, on the other hand, are a special type of array where the dimensions are specified at declaration time and their size cannot change during program execution. Both tools are widely used in COBOL to store and manipulate sets of data efficiently and organized.

In COBOL, you can declare an array or table by specifying the data type and desired size.

For example, to declare a table of integer numbers with a size of 10, you can use the following statement:

```
01 NUMBERS-TABLE PIC 9(5) OCCURS 10 TIMES.
```

This declares a table named "NUMBERS-TABLE" that can hold up to 10 integer numbers, each with a maximum length of 5 digits. It is important to note that the "OCCURS" statement is used to specify how many times a particular element can appear in the table.

Once the table is declared, you can assign values to the elements using the position index. For example, to assign the value 100 to the third element of the table "NUMBERS-TABLE," you can use the following code:

```
MOVE 100 TO NUMBERS-TABLE(3).
```

This stores the value 100 in the third position of the table "NUMBERS-TABLE". You can access the elements of a table using a MOVE operation or by using the element index within square brackets.

You can also use loops and conditions to access and manipulate array elements. For example, you can use a PERFORM loop to iterate through all elements of a table and display them on the screen:

```
PERFORM VARYING I FROM 1 BY 1 UNTIL I > 10
```

```
    DISPLAY "Element " I " : " NUMBERS-
TABLE(I)
END-PERFORM.
```
```

```

This loop iterates through all elements of the "NUMBERS-TABLE" and displays the value of each element along with its position index.

Tables can also be used to manage complex data, such as records or data structures. For example, you can declare a table of records that contains information about company employees:

```

```

```
01 EMPLOYEES-TABLE.
    05 EMPLOYEE-CODE PIC X(5).
    05 EMPLOYEE-NAME PIC X(30).
    05 EMPLOYEE-SALARY PIC 9(7)V99.
```

```

In this case, a table named "EMPLOYEES-TABLE" is declared that contains three fields for each record: the employee code, employee name, and employee salary. You can access each field of a record using dot notation:

```

MOVE "00123" TO EMPLOYEE-CODE(1).

MOVE "Mario Rossi" TO EMPLOYEE-NAME(1).

MOVE 3000.00 TO EMPLOYEE-SALARY(1).

```

In this example, data relating to the first employee is inserted into the "EMPLOYEES-TABLE". Managing a set of records using tables and arrays in COBOL is easy.
```

Furthermore, you can perform search and sorting operations on data stored in tables and arrays. For example, you can use binary search to find a specific element in a sorted table:

```
SET LOW-INDEX TO 1
SET HIGH-INDEX TO 10
SET FOUND TO FALSE

PERFORM UNTIL FOUND OR (LOW-INDEX > HIGH-INDEX)

    SET MID-INDEX TO (LOW-INDEX + HIGH-INDEX) / 2

    IF SEARCH-VALUE EQUALS NUMBERS-TABLE(MID-INDEX)

        MOVE TRUE TO FOUND

    ELSE
```

```
        IF SEARCH-VALUE LESS THAN NUMBERS-TABLE(MID-INDEX)
            SET HIGH-INDEX TO MID-INDEX - 1
        ELSE
            SET LOW-INDEX TO MID-INDEX + 1
        END-IF
    END-IF
END-PERFORM.
```

In this example, a binary search is performed to find the element "SEARCH-VALUE" in the table "NUMBERS-TABLE". The variable "FOUND" is set to TRUE if the element is successfully found.

In conclusion, the use of arrays and tables is essential for organizing and manipulating data in COBOL efficiently and structured. These tools allow for easy management of complex data sets, executing search and sorting operations, and accessing record elements quickly and efficiently. By using arrays and tables, complex algorithms and functionalities can be logically and concretely implemented within COBOL programs.

9. COBOL Development Tools
Development environments for COBOL
Compilation and execution of COBOL
programs Debugging and testing of
COBOL programs

COBOL development tools, development environments, program compilation and execution, as well as program debugging and testing are essential to ensure the efficiency and correctness of applications developed in this language.

COBOL development tools are designed to facilitate the process of creating, modifying, and maintaining COBOL code. These tools provide an integrated environment that includes text editors, compilers, debuggers, and profiling tools to optimize program performance. Some of the most popular tools for COBOL development include Micro Focus Visual COBOL, IBM Enterprise COBOL, and GNU COBOL.

Micro Focus Visual COBOL is a popular development tool that offers an integrated environment for developing COBOL applications on Windows and Linux platforms. This tool includes an advanced text editor with features like code auto-completion and refactoring, a COBOL compiler optimized for efficient code generation, and a debugger for correcting runtime errors. Visual COBOL also supports integration with modern development platforms like Eclipse and Visual Studio, allowing developers to work in a familiar environment.

IBM Enterprise COBOL is another widely-used development tool for creating COBOL applications on IBM mainframe systems. This tool provides a complete development environment that includes a text editor with code analysis features, a high-performance COBOL compiler, and performance monitoring tools to optimize program execution. Enterprise COBOL is designed to integrate with existing technologies on mainframe platforms, enabling developers to create highly scalable and reliable COBOL applications.

GNU COBOL is an open-source implementation of the COBOL language that offers a free and flexible alternative to commercial tools. This tool provides a complete development environment with a configurable text editor, a COBOL compiler compatible with ANSI and ISO standards, and a debugger for analyzing runtime issues. GNU COBOL is supported by an active community of developers who provide regular updates and technical support for users.

COBOL development environments are designed to support the various stages of the software development life cycle, from design to maintenance. These environments provide tools for code management, team collaboration, and automation of development processes. Some of the most advanced development environments for COBOL include IBM Rational Developer for z Systems, CA Endevor, and Micro Focus Application Lifecycle Management.

IBM Rational Developer for z Systems is an integrated development environment designed for creating COBOL applications on IBM mainframe systems. This environment provides tools for visual software modeling, code library management, and team collaboration. Rational Developer for z Systems also supports automated documentation generation and requirement traceability to ensure the quality of the developed software.

CA Endevor is a mainframe-based development environment designed for managing the application life cycle of COBOL applications. This environment provides tools for code version control, release management, and development activity planning. Endevor also supports impact assessment of code changes and software version reconciliation to ensure consistency between development and production environments.

Micro Focus Application Lifecycle Management is a complete development environment designed to support all stages of the software development life cycle, from design to execution. This environment provides tools for requirement management, project planning, and test management. Application Lifecycle Management also supports team collaboration and requirement traceability to ensure the quality and success of development projects.

Compilation and execution of COBOL programs are crucial stages of the development process that transform source code into a functional executable. Compilation is the process by which the COBOL compiler translates the source code into machine language, while execution is the phase in which the program is run and produces the desired output. During the compilation and execution of COBOL programs, it is important to consider factors such as code optimization, system resource management, and software quality.

The compilation process of COBOL programs begins with the compiler scanning the source code to identify any syntax or logic errors. Once the scanning is complete, the compiler translates the source code into machine language using the compilation directives specified in the source code. During the compilation process, the compiler also generates debug information and program symbols to support subsequent debugging and testing.

After completing the COBOL program, it is necessary to run it to verify that it produces the desired output and functions correctly. During the program execution, it is important to monitor the software performance, system resource consumption, and the correctness of the output produced. In case of errors during execution, it is necessary to identify and correct the causes of the problems to ensure the program operates correctly.

Debugging and testing COBOL programs are essential processes to identify and correct errors in the source code and ensure the quality and reliability of the developed applications. Debugging is the process by which developers identify and correct runtime errors in COBOL programs, while testing is the process of verifying the software functionality and performance before release.

During debugging of COBOL programs, developers use debugging tools such as the debugger integrated in the development environment or profiling tools to identify and correct errors in the code. Debugging tools allow developers to run the program step-by-step, monitor program variables, and identify any logic or syntax errors. Once an error is identified, developers can make the necessary code corrections and repeat the debugging process to verify the correctness of the changes.

Testing COBOL programs is a complex process that involves designing and executing tests to verify the software compliance with specified requirements and user expectations. During testing, unit tests, integration tests, functional tests, and performance tests are executed to evaluate the software quality and stability. Unit tests verify the correct operation of individual software components, while integration tests assess the interaction between different components and modules.

Functional tests are designed to verify that the program produces the correct output in response to specific inputs, while performance tests evaluate the software performance in terms of speed, resource usage, and scalability. During COBOL program testing, it is important to consider the test requirements specified in the requirements analysis document and acceptance criteria defined by end users.

Example of debugging a COBOL program:

Suppose we have a COBOL program that calculates the sum of two numbers and displays the result on the screen. Here is an example of the source code:

IDENTIFICATION DIVISION.

PROGRAM-ID. SUM.

DATA DIVISION.

WORKING-STORAGE SECTION.

1 NUMBER1 PIC 9(9).

1 NUMBER2 PIC 9(9).

1 SUM PIC 9(9).

PROCEDURE DIVISION.

DISPLAY 'Enter the first number: '.

ACCEPT NUMBER1.

DISPLAY 'Enter the second number: '.

ACCEPT NUMBER2.

COMPUTE SUM = NUMBER1 + NUMBER2.

DISPLAY 'The sum of the two numbers is: ' SUM.

STOP RUN.

Suppose that during the program execution an error occurs that causes an incorrect result in the sum of numbers. To identify and correct the error, you can use the debugger integrated in the development environment. Here is how the debugging process might look like:

1. Start the program in the development environment debugger.

2. Enter the values of the two numbers (e.g., 5 and 3).

3. Run the program step-by-step to check the variable values.

4. Identify the point where the error occurs in the sum calculation.

5. Correct the error in the code (e.g., NUMBER1 + NUMBER2) with the correct evaluation of the mathematical expression.

6. Run the program again to verify the correctness of the modification.

7. Display the correct result of the sum of numbers on the console.

In this way, the debugging process allows developers to identify and correct errors in the source code to ensure the correct operation of the COBOL program.

Development tools for COBOL, development environments, program compilation and execution, as well as debugging and testing of programs are fundamental to ensure the quality and correctness of applications developed in this language. By using advanced tools and following well-defined development procedures, developers can create reliable and scalable COBOL applications that meet the business and end user needs.

10.File Management in Cobol

File management in Cobol is a fundamental activity for most programs written in this language. Files are used to store data permanently and to allow programs to access this information efficiently. In this guide, we will explore the basic concepts of file management in Cobol, providing practical examples to better understand how this process works.

Types of files in Cobol

In Cobol, there are three main types of files:

- Input files: are files from which the program reads data. For example, an input file could contain information about customers or products.

- Output files: are files where the program

writes data. For example, an output file could contain calculation results or reports.

- I/O files: are files that can be read and written by the program. For example, an I/O file could contain a list of transactions to read and update.

File specifiers in Cobol are defined in the environment division of the program and are associated with a particular file. For example, the following code defines three file specifiers: one for an input file (IN-FILE), one for an output file (OUT-FILE), and one for an I/O file (IO-FILE).

Operations on files in Cobol

Basic file operations in Cobol include opening, closing, reading, and writing. Let's see how to perform these operations using practical examples.

Opening a file

To open a file in Cobol, you need to use the OPEN statement. For example, the following code opens an input file called IN-FILE:

```
OPEN INPUT IN-FILE.
```

Closing a file

To close a file in Cobol, you need to use the CLOSE statement. For example, the following code closes the output file named OUT-FILE:

```
CLOSE OUT-FILE.
```

Reading from a file

To read from a file in Cobol, you need to use the READ statement. For example, the following code reads a line from the input file IN-FILE and stores the data in the variable WS-RECORD:

```
READ IN-FILE INTO WS-RECORD.
```

Writing to a file

To write to a file in Cobol, you need to use the WRITE statement. For example, the following code writes a line to the output file OUT-FILE using the data contained in the variable WS-RECORD:

```
WRITE WS-RECORD INTO OUT-FILE.
```

Practical example of file management in Cobol

To illustrate how file management works in Cobol, let's consider a simple program that reads data from an input file, performs operations on the read data, and writes the results to an output file. Below is an example of Cobol code that implements this scenario:

[Code example is provided]

In this example, the program opens an input file 'input.dat' and an output file 'output.dat'. Subsequently, the program reads data from the input file line by line until it encounters the string 'END'. For each line read, the program performs an operation on the data (in this case, simply concatenating the name and age) and writes the result to the output file. Finally, the program closes both files and terminates execution.

Conclusion

File management is an essential part of programming in Cobol, as it allows programs to access and store data efficiently. By using file specifiers and file operations such as opening, closing, reading, and writing, file management can be easily implemented in Cobol programs. We hope this guide has been helpful in better understanding how file management works in Cobol.

11.Database Management in Cobol

Cobol is a widely used programming language in the business world for data management on mainframes. One of the main tasks of a Cobol program is managing data within a database. Here's how database management can be done in Cobol.

To manage a database in Cobol, a compatible DBMS (Database Management System) must be used, such as DB2, MySQL, or Oracle. These DBMS allow for creating, modifying, and querying databases within a Cobol program.

Connecting to external databases:

To connect to an external database and interact with the data within a Cobol program, specific commands need to be used. Firstly, a configuration section must be defined to allow the program to connect to the external database. This section may contain information such as the database name, username, and password required for database access.

Here is an example of how a connection to an external database could be configured in a Cobol program:

IDENTIFICATION DIVISION.

PROGRAM-ID. DatabaseManagement.

DATA DIVISION.

WORKING-STORAGE SECTION.

01 SQLCA.

05 SQLCODE PIC S9(9) COMP.

05 SQLSTATE PIC X(5).

01 DB2DSN PIC X(8) VALUE 'DATABASE'.

01 USERID PIC X(8) VALUE

'USERNAME'.

01 PASSWORD PIC X(8) VALUE 'PASSWORD'.

01 DSORT-CONNECT SECTION.

EXEC SQL

CONNECT TO :DB2DSN

USER :USERID

USING :PASSWORD.

Once the connection is successfully established, SQL queries can be executed to query the external database and manipulate data within the Cobol program.

Executing SQL queries in Cobol:

To execute an SQL query within a Cobol program, specific EXEC SQL commands are required for inserting, updating, deleting, or querying data in the external database.

Here is an example of how a simple SELECT SQL query can be executed in a Cobol program:

```
PROCEDURE DIVISION.

EXEC SQL

DECLARE C1 CURSOR FOR

SELECT * FROM TABLE;

EXEC SQL

OPEN C1;

EXEC SQL

FETCH C1 INTO :variable1, :variable2;

PERFORM UNTIL SQLCODE = 100

DISPLAY variable1, variable2

EXEC SQL

FETCH C1 INTO :variable1, :variable2;

END-PERFORM.
```

```
EXEC SQL
CLOSE C1.
```

The above code executes a SELECT SQL query that selects all records from the TABLE and displays them on the screen. The code uses a cursor to iterate through the selected records and assigns them to variables variable1 and variable2 for display. Finally, the cursor is closed.

Manipulating data from databases in Cobol programs:

Another common operation within a Cobol program is manipulating data from the database. This can include inserting, updating, and deleting records in the external database.

Here is an example of how a record can be inserted into a table in an external database from a Cobol program:

```
IDENTIFICATION DIVISION.
PROGRAM-ID. DataInsertion.
DATA DIVISION.
WORKING-STORAGE SECTION.
01 WS-VAR1 PIC X(10) VALUE 'VALUE1'.
01 WS-VAR2 PIC X(10) VALUE 'VALUE2'.

PROCEDURE DIVISION.
EXEC SQL
INSERT INTO TABLE (COLUMN1, COLUMN2)
VALUES (:WS-VAR1, :WS-VAR2).
```

The above code inserts a new record into the TABLE of the external database, with the values for columns COLUMN1 and COLUMN2 defined by the variables WS-

VAR1 and WS-VAR2.

In addition to insertion, records can be updated and deleted in the external database using SQL commands within a Cobol program.

In conclusion, database management in Cobol involves connecting to external databases, executing SQL queries to query and manipulate data within the Cobol program, and manipulating data from the database. There are many specific commands and instructions that can be used within a Cobol program to effectively manage data in an external database. Cobol remains one of the most used languages for data management on business mainframes, and its ability to connect and interact with external databases makes it a valuable application for many companies worldwide.

12. Structured Programming in Cobol

Structured programming in COBOL is an approach to writing code that aims to organize and structure the program in a logical and understandable way. This is important because it makes it easier for programmers to work on the code, maintain it, and modify it in the future. Using structured programming in COBOL involves dividing the main program into separate and reusable modules, making maintenance and code reuse easier.

One of the key concepts of structured programming in COBOL is the use of subprograms and functions. These are blocks of code that perform a specific operation and can be called from different parts of the main program. This allows the code to be divided into smaller and more manageable units, making it easier to understand and maintain the program over time.

Subprograms and functions in COBOL can be defined as separate code sections that are called from the main program using a PERFORM or CALL statement. Here is an example of how a subprogram could be defined in COBOL:

The examples above show how it is possible to separate the calculation logic into a separate subprogram and call it from the main program using the PERFORM statement with the use of linkage data. In this case, the CALC-SUM subprogram takes two variables as input and returns the result of their sum.

To write modular and reusable programs in COBOL, it is important to follow some best practices. Here are some tips to do so:

1. Divide the program into logical modules: dividing the code into separate modules for each functionality helps keep the code organized and easily manageable. Each

module should perform a single specific and clear function.

2. Use subprograms and functions: separating the calculation logic into subprograms and functions makes the code more readable and easier to maintain. It also allows you to reuse the same logic in multiple parts of the program.

3. Use meaningful names for variables and procedures: giving descriptive names to variables and procedures helps understand the code more easily and reduces the risk of errors.

4. Comment the code: adding comments to the code to explain the logic behind the operations and choices implemented. This makes it easier for other programmers to understand the code and helps in future maintenance.

5. Avoid duplicate code: try to minimize code duplication by writing reusable functions and subprograms. This makes the code more efficient and easier to maintain.

6. Use control structures correctly: use IF, PERFORM, EVALUATE statements appropriately to manage the program flow in a clear and understandable way.

Structured programming in COBOL is a fundamental approach to developing modular, reusable, and easy-to-maintain programs. Following the best practices listed above helps programmers write quality and well-structured code that can be easily understood and modified in the future.

13.Object-oriented programming in Cobol

Object-oriented programming (OOP) is a programming methodology based on the concept of "objects," which can contain data in the form of attributes and behaviors in the form of methods. In this way, the code is organized into logical units that represent real-world concepts, making it easier for design, maintenance, and code reuse.

In COBOL, one of the longest-standing and popular programming languages used in the mainframe field, object-oriented programming was introduced with version 4.2 of the language, with support for classes and objects. However, COBOL is not a natively object-oriented language like Java or C++, so the implementation of object-oriented programming is limited compared to other languages.

In object-oriented languages like Java or C++,

key concepts include inheritance, encapsulation, and polymorphism. In COBOL, on the other hand, object orientation is primarily based on classes and objects, with syntax and semantics similar to more traditional languages like PL/I.

Classes in COBOL consist of data (fields) and procedures (operations or methods) that operate on this data. Objects, which are instances of a class, contain specific data and field values, and can call class methods to manipulate this data.

The creation of classes and objects in COBOL is done by declaring complex data structures using the language's groups and records. The BLOCK CONTAINS attribute in the data section declaration indicates that the section contains a class and defines some other properties of the class. The class behavior is defined within the PROCEDURES DIVISION, with the definition of methods operating on the class data.

An example of a class declaration in COBOL could be:

```
IDENTIFICATION DIVISION.
PROGRAM-ID. SampleProgram.

ENVIRONMENT DIVISION.

DATA DIVISION.

WORKING-STORAGE SECTION.
01 BookClass.
   05 Title PIC X(30).
   05 Author PIC X(20).
   05 Price PIC 9(5)V99.
   05 QtyInStock PIC 9(4) COMP.
```

```
01 BookObject BASED ON BookClass.
PROCEDURE DIVISION.


MOVE 'The Great Gatsby' TO BookObject::Title
MOVE 'F. Scott Fitzgerald' TO BookObject::Author
MOVE 19.99 TO BookObject::Price
MOVE 100 TO BookObject::QtyInStock.
```

In this example, BookClass is the class declaration representing a book, with attributes such as title, author, price, and quantity in stock. BookObject is an instance of the BookClass class, containing specific values for a specific book.

Class methods can be defined in the PROCEDURE DIVISION section and called from outside to manipulate class objects. For example, a method to check if a book is in stock could be defined as follows:

```
01 CheckStock.
    MOVE ZERO TO RETURN-CODE
    IF BookObject::QtyInStock = 0
    MOVE 1 TO RETURN-CODE.
```

This method checks if the book represented by the BookObject object is in stock and sets the return code to 1 if it is not available.

One of the advantages of object-oriented programming in COBOL is the increased modularity of the code and ease of maintenance. By defining data and behaviors related to a specific concept in a separate class, it is easier to manage and modify the code without making changes to other parts of the program.

Object-oriented programming in COBOL also offers the ability to reuse code more effectively. By creating classes that represent generic and reusable concepts, it is possible to create new objects that inherit behaviors and properties of existing classes, saving time and effort in writing code.

However, there are also some disadvantages to object-oriented programming in COBOL. Support for advanced OOP concepts such as inheritance and polymorphism is limited compared to other languages, making it more complex to implement certain design patterns or class structures.

Additionally, object-oriented programming in COBOL may not be the best choice for all types of projects. For simpler applications or legacy projects that do not require complex code structuring, it may be more convenient to use a traditional procedural approach rather than adopting an object-oriented paradigm.

In conclusion, object-oriented programming in COBOL offers greater flexibility and modularity in code, allowing for better management and maintenance of software. Although it has some limitations compared to more advanced OOP languages, it is still possible to leverage the benefits of OOP in COBOL to improve code quality and efficiency.

14. COBOL Code Optimization

COBOL, short for Common Business Oriented Language, is a programming language developed for processing commercial and business data. Despite being considered "dated" compared to other more modern technologies, it is still widely used in many companies, especially in the financial and banking sector, where numerous legacy systems are written in COBOL.

Over the years, COBOL systems tend to accumulate obsolete, redundant, and inefficient code, which can cause program performance slowdowns and make software maintenance and updates more difficult. For this reason, it is necessary to adopt COBOL code optimization techniques to improve program performance and ensure more efficient and stable operation.

COBOL code optimization techniques can be

divided into different categories, including:

1. Code simplification: eliminate redundant code, adequately comment the code to make the programming logic clearer, and reduce the complexity of instructions to facilitate program understanding.

2. Use of optimized control structures: use control structures like IF-ELSE, PERFORM, EVALUATE efficiently to minimize the number of instructions and improve code readability.

3. Correct use of variables: assign variables correctly and avoid declaring unused or redundant variables to reduce memory space usage and improve program performance.

4. Use of conditional statements: correctly use conditional statements to control program flow efficiently, avoiding infinite loops or

redundant instructions that can cause performance slowdowns.

5. SQL query optimization: if the COBOL program uses SQL queries to interact with a database, it is important to optimize queries to improve program performance and ensure quick data retrieval.

To successfully implement these COBOL code optimization techniques, it is essential to use specific code profiling tools that help identify critical areas of the program that require intervention to improve performance.

Some common tools for COBOL code profiling include:

1. IBM Application Performance Analyzer for z/OS: this tool allows you to analyze COBOL code to identify execution time intervals and pinpoint areas that require optimization to

improve performance.

2. Compuware Strobe: this software is designed to analyze COBOL application performance and identify critical points that require optimization to reduce execution times.

3. Micro Focus Visual COBOL Analyzer: this tool suite offers advanced features for COBOL code analysis, allowing you to identify areas for potential optimization and performance improvement.

4. CA Mainframe Application Tuner: this software provides comprehensive features for analyzing COBOL application performance and helps identify performance slowdown issues and propose solutions to improve them.

By using these tools and applying the described COBOL code optimization techniques, significant improvements can be made to COBOL program performance, ensuring more efficient and reliable operation of legacy systems. Additionally, optimizing COBOL code can help reduce maintenance and management costs of legacy systems, ensuring optimal operation of business applications.

15. COBOL Syntax

The syntax, although it may seem dated compared to more recent programming languages, is extremely powerful and flexible, allowing for the creation of complex and efficient programs.

COBOL is a declarative language, which means that the programmer declares which operations need to be executed and does not have to worry about how these operations are actually carried out by the computer. This feature makes it particularly suitable for writing business programs, where it is important to focus on rules and business logic rather than specific computer operations.

The syntax of COBOL is based on a set of well-defined and structured rules that define how commands and instructions should be written and organized within a program. For example, every line of code in COBOL must start with a sequence number indicating the relative position of the line in the program. This sequence number also helps facilitate the reading and modification of the code, allowing for the insertion of new lines or changes in order without having to rewrite the entire program.

In addition to the sequence number, each line of code in COBOL is composed of a series of keywords and identifiers that indicate the instructions to be carried out and the variables involved in the process. For example, to declare a variable in COBOL, the keyword "PIC" is used followed by the data type of the variable and its length. For instance, to declare an integer variable with a length of 5 digits, the following syntax is used:

```
01 NUMBER PIC 9(5).
```

In this example, "NUMBER" is the name of the variable, "PIC" indicates the data type (in this case an integer), and "9(5)" specifies the length of the variable (5 digits). It is important to note that in COBOL, variables must be declared at the beginning of the program within a specific section called "SECTION DATA DIVISION" in order to be used later in the code.

In addition to variable declaration, COBOL syntax includes a wide range of instructions and commands for handling input/output, mathematical calculations, conditional decisions, and iteration loops. For example, to perform arithmetic calculations in COBOL, the "ADD" and "MULTIPLY" instructions are used followed by the names of the variables involved:

```
```

ADD NUMBER-1 TO NUMBER-2.

MULTIPLY NUMBER-1 BY 10 GIVING

RESULT.
```



These commands respectively perform an addition between two variables and a multiplication between a variable and a constant value. It is important to note that in COBOL, arithmetic operations are performed precisely and in accordance with standard mathematical rules, ensuring accurate and reliable results.


In addition to arithmetic operations, COBOL syntax also includes instructions for handling conditional decisions and iteration loops. For example, to execute a conditional statement in COBOL, the "IF" statement is used followed by a condition to be checked and the instructions to be executed in case of truth or falsehood of the condition:


```

```
IF NUMBER-1 IS GREATER THAN
NUMBER-2

   DISPLAY "The first number is greater than
the second."

ELSE

   DISPLAY "The second number is greater
than the first."

END-IF.
```

In this example, the condition that the value of the variable "NUMBER-1" is greater than the value of the variable "NUMBER-2" is checked, and an appropriate output message is displayed depending on the result of the check. "ELSE IF" and "ELSE" statements can also be used to handle multiple conditions within a single conditional statement.

Regarding iteration loops, COBOL includes the "PERFORM" and "UNTIL" instructions that allow for a block of instructions to be repeated until a certain condition is met:

```
PERFORM UNTIL COUNTER IS GREATER THAN 10
   ADD 1 TO COUNTER
   DISPLAY "The counter is " COUNTER
END-PERFORM.
```

In this example, the block of instructions is repeatedly executed until the value of the variable "COUNTER" exceeds 10. This type of construct is particularly useful for handling calculation or input/output operations that need to be repeated multiple times within a program.

In addition to basic instructions for data

management and flow control, COBOL also includes a wide range of advanced features that allow for the creation of complex and scalable programs. For example, COBOL supports the use of arrays and structured records to effectively and organizedly handle complex data. It also includes standard libraries and modules that allow for the reuse of previously written code and the easy integration of new features within an existing program.

COBOL syntax is essential for writing efficient and reliable programs in the business and commercial application sectors. Although it may seem dated compared to more recent programming languages, COBOL is still widely used in many companies and institutions worldwide for its power, flexibility, and reliability. With a solid understanding of COBOL syntax and its advanced features, it is possible to create sophisticated and scalable programs that effectively meet the needs of the modern business world.

16. Example of COBOL Application

COBOL (Common Business Oriented Language) is a high-level programming language designed primarily for data management, business transactions, and financial calculations. Despite being one of the oldest languages still in use, COBOL is still used in many sectors, especially in the financial and governmental worlds.

Here is an example of a COBOL application that calculates an employee's gross salary based on the hours worked and the hourly rate.

```
```

IDENTIFICATION DIVISION.

PROGRAM-ID. Salary_Calculation.

DATA DIVISION.

WORKING-STORAGE SECTION.

01 Employee.

   05 Name   PIC X(20).

   05 Surname   PIC X(20).

   05 Hours_Worked   PIC 9(3).

   05 Hourly_Rate   PIC 9(5)V99.

   05 Taxes   PIC 9(5)V99.

   05 Gross_Salary   PIC 9(5)V99.

PROCEDURE DIVISION.

BEGIN.

   DISPLAY "Enter employee's name: ".

   ACCEPT Name.

   DISPLAY "Enter employee's surname: ".

   ACCEPT Surname.

   DISPLAY "Enter hours worked: ".

   ACCEPT Hours_Worked.

```
    DISPLAY "Enter hourly rate: ".

    ACCEPT Hourly_Rate.


    COMPUTE Gross_Salary = Hours_Worked * Hourly_Rate.

    COMPUTE Taxes = Gross_Salary * 0.2.

    DISPLAY "The gross salary of ", Name, Surname, " is: ", Gross_Salary.

    DISPLAY "Taxes to be paid are: ", Taxes.
END.
    STOP RUN.
```

In this example, the first section (IDENTIFICATION DIVISION) specifies the program name, while the DATA DIVISION section defines the variables used in the program.

The WORKING-STORAGE SECTION defines the employee's data structure, including name, surname, hours worked, hourly rate, gross salary, and taxes.

In the PROCEDURE DIVISION section, the BEGIN procedure prompts the user to enter the employee's name, surname, hours worked, and hourly rate. The program then calculates the gross salary by multiplying the hours worked by the hourly rate and calculates the taxes as 20% of the gross salary.

Finally, the program displays the gross salary and taxes to be paid for the specified employee.

This is just a simple example of how COBOL can be used to write an application for salary management. COBOL is a versatile language that can be used for a wide range of business and financial applications. While less common than more modern languages, COBOL still plays an important role in the business and technology world.

Index

1. Introduction to COBOL pg.4

2. Structure of a COBOL program pg.8

3. Declaration of variables in COBOL pg.11

4. Program control structures (if, else, do, etc.) in COBOL pg.18

5. Use of comments in COBOL code pg.27

6. Declaration and usage of various types of data (alpha, numeric, decimal, etc.) in COBOL pg.31

7. Data Manipulation in COBOL pg.38

8. Using arrays and tables in COBOL pg.47

9. COBOL Development Tools Development environments for COBOL Compilation and execution of COBOL programs Debugging and testing of COBOL programs pg.55

10. File Management in Cobol pg.67

11. Database Management in Cobol pg.73

12. Structured Programming in Cobol pg.80

13. Object-oriented programming in Cobol pg.84

14. COBOL Code Optimization pg.91

15. COBOL Syntax pg.96

16. Example of COBOL Application pg.104

www.ingramcontent.com/pod-product-compliance
Lightning Source LLC
Chambersburg PA
CBHW050317230526
45471CB00005B/2225